# GETTING STARTED

Sewing is a fun and exciting craft activity, and an easy one to master – all it involves is joining pieces of fabric together with a needle and thread! This book will introduce you to the essential skills you'll need to get into sewing by hand.

There are 11 projects to try in this book, with clear instructions to help you get the techniques right. Each one will teach you new skills: just practise your stitches a few times and you'll soon be ready to start an exciting project!

When you're ready to take your sewing a step further, you'll find some great ideas for more challenging activities at the back of the book.

The great thing about sewing is that you can make your creations exactly the way you want them. You're in charge – so let your creativity run wild! Once you've started, there'll be no stopping you – you'll be itching to stitch!

# SEWING KIT ESSENTIALS

All you need to get started with sewing is some fabric and a simple sewing kit. It can all be found in haberdashery shops or departments.

## FABRIC

**COTTON** This fabric is soft but feels nice and crisp. This makes it easy to mark with chalk, cut out and sew.

**FELT** A soft fabric that doesn't fray and is easy to cut into shapes, so you can use the smallest scraps.

**PINKING SHEARS** The zigzag edge of these scissors helps prevent fabric from fraying.

**EMBROIDERY THREAD** Used for decorative stitching and working with felt, embroidery thread comes in 'skeins' made of six strands. Use one or two strands when working with delicate fabrics, and three or four strands when working with felt.

Don't use your dressmaking scissors to cut paper as it could blunt them.

**SCISSORS** Use dressmaking scissors with longer blades for cutting out fabric and smaller ones for snipping threads.

**NEEDLES** Buy a pack of needles with different sized holes (called 'eyes') so you can choose the best one for the project.

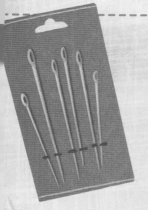

**PINS** Pins are handy for keeping your fabric in place while you sew it.

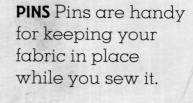

**CHALK PENCIL** Use this to mark lines on fabric before cutting it. The chalk marks can be wiped off when you've finished the project.

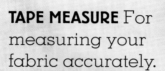

**THREAD** Ordinary sewing thread comes on a spool and is used for joining cotton fabric together.

**TAPE MEASURE** For measuring your fabric accurately.

BBON OR WEBBING ood for making ndles or ties.

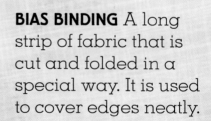

**BIAS BINDING** A long strip of fabric that is cut and folded in a special way. It is used to cover edges neatly.

**TOY FILLING** A lightweight material used for projects requiring shape.

**BUTTONS** Add them to your projects for a pop of colour!

**CUSHION INSERT** To fill cushion covers.

# STITCHES AND TECHNIQUES

All of the stitches in this book are simple to do. Take your time and don't worry if your stitches are not all the same size – it will add to the handmade feel of the project!

**THREADING A NEEDLE** Cut the end of the thread so it has a blunt edge. Gently push the thread through the eye of the needle, then take hold of it from the other side and pull through.

**STARTING YOUR WORK** Make a knot in one end of your thread. When you start to sew, bring your needle through the fabric so that the knot lies on the WRONG side.

**FINISHING YOUR WORK** Take the needle through to the WRONG side of the fabric. Make a small stitch, but don't pull the thread tight, just leave a loop. Bring the needle back through the loop to form a knot. Repeat once more, then cut the thread close to the knot.

Fabric usually has a 'RIGHT side' (the side you want to show off) and a 'WRONG side'.

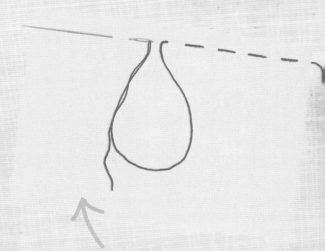

## RUNNING STITCH

Used to lightly hold pieces of fabric together. Bring the needle through the fabric, then make a stitch by putting the needle through the fabric a short distance away. Bring your needle back up, the same distance as the first stitch. Continue weaving your needle in and out of the fabric to create a dashed line of even stitches.

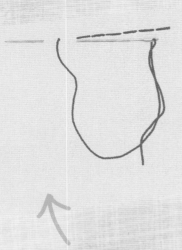

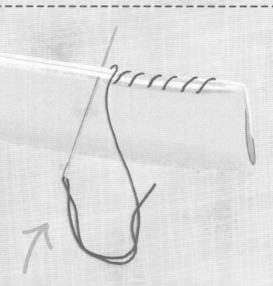

## BACK-STITCH

For holding pieces of fabric together securely. Make two running stitches, then bring the needle back to the end of the first stitch. Bring it out again one stitch ahead. Continue.

## OVERCAST OR OVERSTITCH

Used to sew two edges together. Bring the needle out to one side of the fabric. Push it back through both edges of the fabric, then out again a bit further along the seam. Continue until the gap is closed.

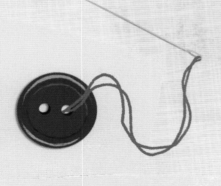

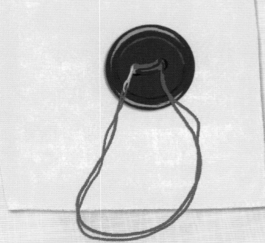

## SEWING ON A BUTTON

Thread your needle and knot your thread. Place the button on your work and bring your needle up from the WRONG side of the fabric through one of the button holes. Push the needle back through the other hole. Pull the thread tight, then go back through the two holes a few times to secure. Finish with a back-stitch and knot on the WRONG side.

# LAVENDER BAG

Lavender bags are fun to make and are a great way to practise your running stitch.

## STEP 1

Cut out two 12-cm squares of fabric and trim the edges with pinking shears.

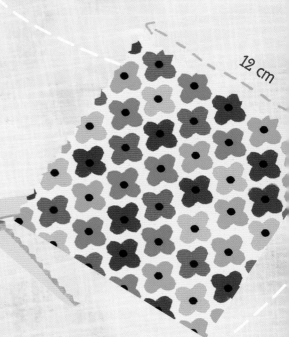

12 cm

## YOU WILL NEED

Pinking shears

Cotton fabric

Thread

Pins

Needle

Teaspoon

Lavender

Scissors

Tape measure

## STEP 2

Pin the two squares together with the RIGHT sides facing out.

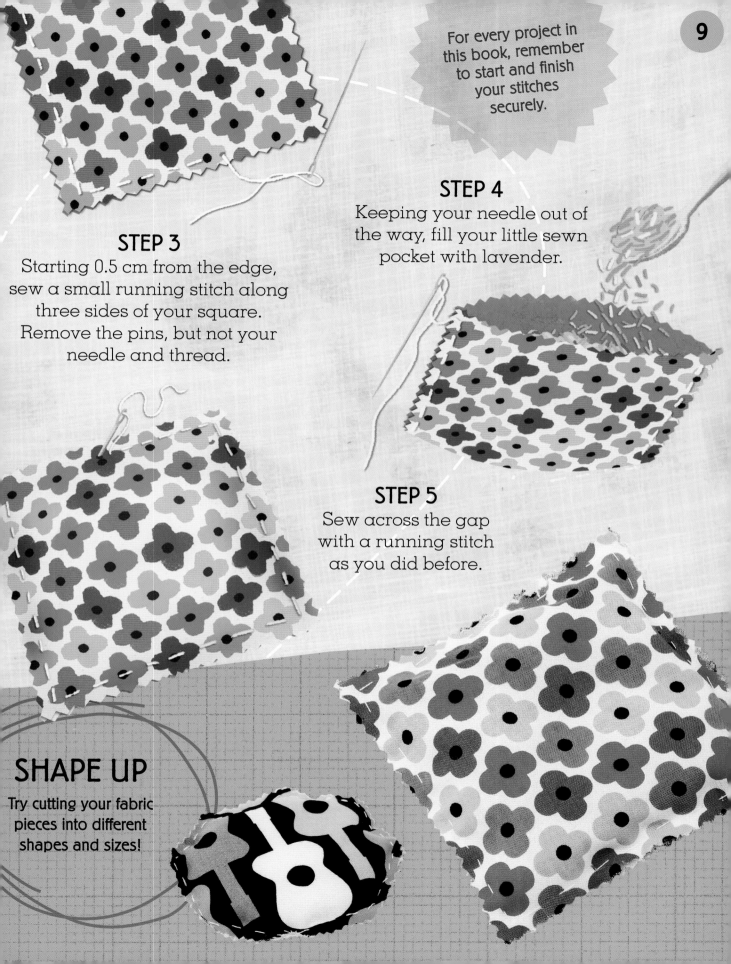

For every project in this book, remember to start and finish your stitches securely.

## STEP 3
Starting 0.5 cm from the edge, sew a small running stitch along three sides of your square. Remove the pins, but not your needle and thread.

## STEP 4
Keeping your needle out of the way, fill your little sewn pocket with lavender.

## STEP 5
Sew across the gap with a running stitch as you did before.

## SHAPE UP
Try cutting your fabric pieces into different shapes and sizes!

# FUNKY FELT FLOWER

Choose a thread colour that contrasts with your felt colours to really show off your running stitch.

## STEP 1

Trace the two flower templates from the back of the book on to tracing paper and cut out.

## YOU WILL NEED

Scraps of felt in two different colours

Button

Tracing paper

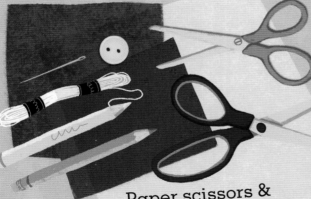

Needle

Paper scissors & sewing scissors

Embroidery thread

Pencil

Chalk pencil

## STEP 2

Place the larger flower templa on to your first scrap of felt an draw around it with your chal pencil. Cut out the large flowe then repeat the process with th smaller flower template and the second piece of felt.

# STEP 3

Sew a running stitch round the edge of each of the two flower shapes.

Don't forget to use three or four strands of embroidery thread when working with felt.

# STEP 4

Lay the small flower on top of the large flower and place your button on top. Sew the button on to the middle of the flowers through both layers of felt.

Don't forget to wipe the chalk marks your fabric!

# LOWER POWER

Try making a flower with three layers instead of two!

# BUNTING

Bunting always brightens up a room, so why not make some for your bedroom?

## YOU WILL NEED

Cotton fabric (at least two different colours or patterns)

Scissors

Pinking shears

Pencil

Chalk pencil

Thin card

Needle and thread

Tape measure

Pins

1-metre pack of bias binding

## STEP 1

Make a triangle template from ca
The short side should be 10 cm and
two longer sides 15 cm each. Dra
around your template on to your fi
fabric six times, then draw another
triangles on the second fabric.

## STEP 2

Cut out your triangles. Use
normal scissors for the shor
side, but cut the long sides
with pinking shears to
prevent them from fraying

## STEP 4
Unfold the bias binding and mark 15 cm from one end with a pin. Place a flag at this point, then fold the binding down so that the top edge is covered. Pin in place.

## STEP 3
With the RIGHT sides facing out, match up two triangles of the same fabric to make each flag. Lay your flags out in the order you'd like.

## STEP 5
Pin the flags 2 cm apart, checking that both sides of the flag are sandwiched between the binding. Pin the tail edges together too.

## STEP 6
Sew all the way along the bias binding with a running stitch, removing your pins as you get to them. Make sure you sew through the flags and bias binding together.

## COLOUR CONTRAST
Try using bias binding in a different colour or pattern from the fabric to create a contrast.

# HANGING DECORATION

Use a biscuit cutter to make a hanging decoration!

## STEP 1

Draw around your biscuit cutter on to your felt twice, and cut out both pieces.

## YOU WILL NEED

Gingerbread-man biscuit cutter

18-cm length of ribbon

Chalk pencil

Hole punch

Embroidery thread

Toy filling

Brown felt

Needle   Pins
Two buttons

Small scrap of black felt   Scissors

## STEP 2

Cut out two eyes from your black f[...]
using a hole punch. Sew the eyes [...]
one of the felt shapes with one o[...]
two small back-stitches. Sew tw[...]
buttons to the middle
of the same shape.

## STEP 3

Draw a smile on your gingerbread man's face and sew over it using back-stitch.

## STEP 4

Fold your ribbon in half and sandwich it between the two felt shapes, about 1 cm from the top. Pin the ribbon and the two shapes together.

## STEP 5

Sew a running stitch all the way around the shape. Pause about three-quarters of the way round. Put toy filling inside the shape, poking it into the nooks and crannies. Be careful not to strain the stitches! Continue sewing the gap closed with a running stitch.

## DOUBLE UP

Sew a smaller layer of felt to the top layer with an overcast stitch before sewing the decoration together.

# PURR-FECT PHONE HOLDER

Personalise a phone holder with a fun fabric picture.

## STEP 1

Put your phone on the felt a mark 1 cm past each side of phone's width with chalk. Fo the felt over your phone ar mark 1 cm past the top of th phone with chalk. Cut out the felt following your chalk guides.

## YOU WILL NEED

Embroidery thread

Pencil

Felt for phone case

Paper scissors

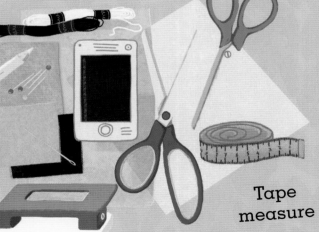

Tape measure

Sewing scissors

Needle

Phone

Tracing paper

Chalk pencil

Hole punch

Felt scraps for cat's head, eyes and nose

## STEP 2

Trace the cat template from the back of this book on to tracing paper and cut it out. Draw arour it on to your cat's head felt and c out. Cut two small black circles f eyes using a hole punch, and c pink triangle for the nose.

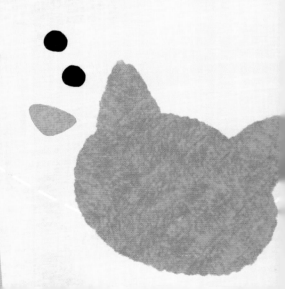

## STEP 3

Sew the eyes and nose in place with a few small stitches. Draw some whiskers and a mouth and sew over this line with black thread using back-stitch.

## STEP 4

Fold the phone case felt in half and carefully pin the cat to the top layer of felt only. Unfold your felt.

## STEP 6

Fold the felt in half and pin the two halves together. Sew down each side using overcast stitch, then remove the pins.

## STEP 5

Using an overcast stitch, stitch the cat to the felt.

## OINK

Use the same template to make a pig! Use pink felt and sew on a button for its snout.

# SHIRT CUSHION

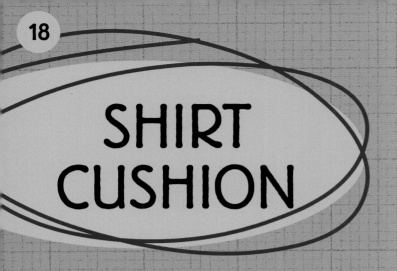

Work your sewing magic on an old shirt and transform it into a stylish cushion cover!

## YOU WILL NEED

Chalk pencil   Scissors   Pins   Needle

A 35 cm x 35 cm cushion insert

An old shirt with buttons on the front

Thread

Tape measure

Iron

## STEP 1

Button the shirt up and draw a 32-cm line across the front. Place pin either end of the line, going through sides of the shirt. Make sure the butt are in the middle of the line.

## STEP 2

Draw a 32-cm line down from each end of the horizontal line a join to form a square. Add pin at each corner, through both sides of the shirt.

## STEP 3
Cut this square out through both layers of the shirt and remove the pins.

## STEP 4
Place the two squares together with WRONG sides facing out (with buttons on the inside) and pin.

## STEP 6
Undo the buttons and turn your cushion cover RIGHT side out. Poke the corners out gently and iron the cushion cover (ask an adult to help you). Insert your cushion pad and do the buttons up.

## STEP 5
tarting 1 cm from the edge, sew around all four sides with a back-stitch.

## PICK POCKETS
Choose a shirt with pockets - then your cushion will have pockets too!

# ALPHABET KEY RING

These super-cute key rings make great gifts!

## YOU WILL NEED

Embroidery thread

8-cm length of ribbon

Needle

Mug or cup

Paper

Pins

Sewing scissors and paper scissors

Chalk pencil

Key ring attachment

Small pieces of felt in two colours

Toy filling

## STEP 1

Draw around the mug on to the first colour of felt twice, and cut out two pieces.

## STEP 2

Print out or draw a capital letter to fit in the middle of these circles and cut out. Draw around the letter on to the other colour of felt and cut out.

For letters with holes in the middle (such as A, B and D), sew the middle section first, then sew around the outside.

## STEP 3

Pin the letter to the middle of one of the felt circles and sew in place with a running stitch.

## STEP 4

Fold your ribbon in half and sandwich it between the two felt circles, about 1 cm from the top. Pin the ribbon, then pin the circles together.

## STEP 5

Sew a running stitch all the way round the circle. Pause about three-quarters of the way round.

## STEP 6

Put toy filling inside the circles, then sew the gap closed with a running stitch. Attach a key ring to your ribbon loop.

## SPOTS AND STRIPES

Use a fun printed fabric for your letter for a different look.

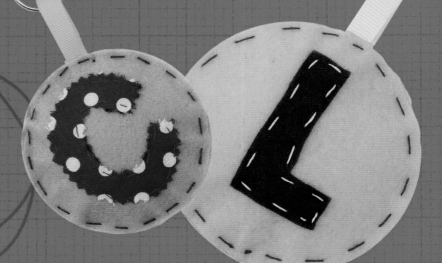

# PENCIL ROLL

This project will make a roll to fit eight pens or pencils.

## STEP 1

Trim the edges of the felt and fabri pieces with pinking shears. Fold th cotton fabric in half lengthways wit the fold at the top – this will be you pocket. On the RIGHT side of the fabric, draw a vertical line 4 cm from the left edge. Repeat for the right-hand edge.

## YOU WILL NEED

60-cm-long piece of ribbon

Embroidery thread

Pinking shears

Chalk pencil

Needle

Tape measure

Scissors

Pins

2 pieces of felt measuring 20 cm x 26 cm

1 piece of cotton fabric measuring 24 cm x 26 cm

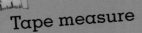

## STEP 2

Draw another vertical line 3 cm from the line you drew on the left. Repeat fou more times – you should hav seven lines in total.

## STEP 4

Place the felt piece with the pocket on top of the second felt piece. Fold the ribbon in half and tuck the folded end in between the two pieces of felt, just above the top of the pocket. Pin everything together.

## STEP 3

Place the pocket on top of the rst felt piece, lining up the bottom edges, and pin in place. Using back-stitch, sew down each titching line, through both layers of cotton and the felt.

## STEP 5

Starting 1 cm from the edge, sew a running stitch around all four sides, making sure you stitch through all the layers. Remove all the pins. Now it's time to add some pencils!

## BRILLIANT BORDER

Add some ribbon to the edges when you sew the layers together to create a pretty border.

# EASY TOTE BAG

Choose a bright, contrasting colour for the handles to make your tote bag really stand out!

## STEP 1

Trim the edges of your fabric with pinking shears. On the RIGHT s[ide] of your fabric, measure 8 cm from th[e] top-left corner along the top edge an[d] mark with your chalk pencil. Do th[e] same on the top-right corner, then rep[eat] for your second piece of fabric.

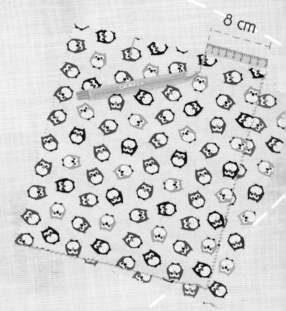

8 cm

## YOU WILL NEED

Pinking shears

2 pieces of cotton fabric measuring 30 cm x 36 cm

Scissors     Iron

Pins

Tape measure

Needle & thread

Chalk pencil

2 pieces of 2.5-cm-wide webbing or ribbon, measuring 50 cm each

## STEP 2

Fold 1 cm of webbing under itself and pin to the first mark. Th[en] pin the other end of the webbing [to] the second mark, again with 1 c[m] folded under. Repeat with the ot[her] piece of fabric and webbing.

## STEP 4

Turn the fabric pieces over to their WRONG sides. Fold the top edge over by 2 cm and pin. Iron this fold into place to give a crisp edge. (Ask an adult for help.)

## STEP 3

Sew both handles down with a back-stitch and remove the pins.

## STEP 5

Secure the handles even more with a back-stitch near the top of the fabric fold. Then stitch along the bottom of the fold with a small running stitch.

## STEP 6

Put the two pieces of fabric on top of each other with WRONG sides facing out and pin. Starting 1 cm from the edge, sew along all three sides of the bag using a back-stitch. Turn your bag the right way round.

## LITTLE AND LARGE

You can make this bag smaller or larger. A tiny tote would make a gorgeous gift bag!

# DRAWSTRING BAG

This useful drawstring bag is perfect for holding all your bits and pieces.

## STEP 1

Trim the edges of your fabric with pinking shears.

## YOU WILL NEED

Polka-dotted fabric measuring 28 cm x 72 cm

Pinking shears

Pins

Iron

Scissors

Chalk pencil

Safety pin

Needle
Thread

Tape measure

Ribbon measuring 85 cm

## STEP 2

On the WRONG side of your fabr measure 5 cm down from the to edge at each side and mark. Joi the two marks with a line. Do th same on the bottom edge.

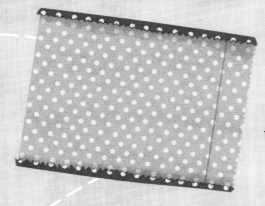

## STEP 3
Fold the fabric in half lengthways so the WRONG sides face out and pin. Starting at the chalk line, sew down each side using a back-stitch. Remove the pins.

## STEP 4
Fold the edges over at the stitch line and iron so they lie closed (ask an adult to help).

## STEP 5
Fold (or iron) down the top of the bag until the bag edge lines up with the chalk line. Pin. Repeat for the other side.

## STEP 6
Stitch along the bottom of the fold with a running stitch. Repeat on the other side of the bag. Remove the pins.

## STEP 7
Secure a safety pin to the end of the ribbon. Feed it through one tunnel, across the gap and through the other tunnel. Remove the safety pin. Make both ends of your ribbon the same length, then tie the ends together.

# PICTURE IT
Make the bag in a plain fabric and sew a picture to the front before sewing the sides together.

# JUGGLING BALL

Juggling balls are fun to sew and are a really unusual gift idea!

## YOU WILL NEED

Felt scraps in four different colours

Paper scissors
Sewing scissors
Tracing paper

Pins

Pencil

Chalk pencil

Needle

Teaspoon

Embroidery thread

80 g dried lentils or rice, for filling

## STEP 1

Trace the juggling ball template from the back of the book and cut out. Pin this shape to a scrap of felt and cut around it. Repeat for the other felt scraps.

## STEP 2

Lightly draw a cross with a chalk pencil on one side of each of your four felt shapes. The side with the cross will be the WRONG side.

## STEP 3

Lay one shape on top of another with the WRONG sides facing out and pin. Sew along one curved edge using a small overcast stitch. Remove the pins.

## STEP 4

Unfold what you've just sewn so that you have the RIGHT sides facing you. Place the third shape on top of the second shape with RIGHT sides facing. Pin, stitch and unpin as before, then repeat with the final shape. You should now have an inside-out juggling ball, all stitched together apart from one gap.

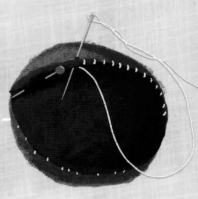

## STEP 5

Pin the RIGHT sides of the two unlinked shapes together. All the sides you can see should have crosses on them to show that they're the WRONG sides.

## STEP 6

Partly stitch the last shapes together, then unpin and turn the shape inside out. Using a teaspoon, fill the ball with lentils or rice until it's nice and plump.

## STEP 7

Pin the edges together and sew closed using an overcast stitch. Unpin.

## TRIPLE IT

Now that you've successfully made one juggling ball, why not make two more for a complete set?

# NEXT STEPS

Now that you've completed the projects in this book, you should feel quite at home with a needle and thread.

## CUSTOMISE YOUR CLOTHES

Expand your hand-sewing skills by having a go at customising. Cut out fabric or felt shapes and stitch them to your clothes for an individual look.

## BEGINNER SEWING CLASSES

If you are feeling confident and would like to take your sewing a step further, you may be ready to start sewing on a machine.

Look out for classes in your area, which are often run by local schools, councils or community centres. A beginner sewing class should teach you how to set up and thread a sewing machine, as well as how to sew in a straight line.

All of the projects from this book that include straight lines of running stitch or back-stitch can also be completed on a sewing machine.

## JOIN A SEWING CLUB

Sewing clubs are often held in specialist sewing schools or craft cafés, and are a great way to meet other sewing fans. They may also offer introductory sewing lessons or classes.

## SIMPLE GARMENT SEWING

If you enjoy using a sewing machine, then why not have a go at making your own clothes? A good first garment to make is a pair of pyjama bottoms – lots of places offer this kind of class, as pyjamas are easy to fit and sew!

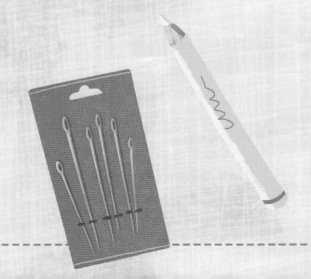

# GLOSSARY

**CUSTOMISE** To change something to your own personal taste.

**FRAY** When a cut edge of fabric unravels or wears away.

**GARMENT** A piece of clothing.

**HABERDASHERY** Small items used in sewing, such as buttons, zips and thread.

**RIGHT SIDE** The side of the fabric that you want to be seen.

**TEMPLATE** Paper or card used as a guide to make copies of shapes.

**TRACE** To copy a pattern or drawing using thin paper (tracing paper) that you can see through.

**TRIM** To cut off the edges of fabric with scissors.

**WRONG SIDE** The side of the fabric that you don't want to be seen.

# USEFUL WEBSITES

## COTTON FABRIC

minervacrafts.com
sewscrumptious.co.uk
elephantinmyhandbag.com
fabricrehab.co.uk

## FELT

abakhan.co.uk
bloomingfelt.co.uk

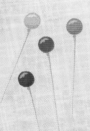

## HABERDASHERY AND CRAFT SUPPLIES

hobbycraft.co.uk
weaverdee.com

## DRIED LAVENDER

provencelavender.co.uk

## CUSHION INSERTS

dunelm.com
IKEA or any homeware shop

# INDEX

Published in Great Britain in 2018 by Wayland

Copyright © Wayland, 2016

All rights reserved.

Editor: Liza Miller
Designer: Simon Daley
Illustration: Esther van den Berg
Photography: Simon Pask Photography

ISBN: 978 0 7502 9195 8

10 9 8 7 6 5 4 3 2 1

Wayland
An imprint of
Hachette Children's Group
Part of Hodder & Stoughton
Carmelite House
50 Victoria Embankment
London EC4Y 0DZ

An Hachette UK Company
www.hachette.co.uk
www.hachettechildrens.co.uk

Printed in China

The website addresses (URLs) included in this book were valid at the time of going to press. However, it is possible that contents or addresses may have changed since the publication of this book. No responsibility for any such changes can be accepted by either the author or the Publisher.